HORRIBLE HISTORIES

THE STORMIN' NORMANS

TERRY DEARY

Illustrated by
Martin Brown

To John Goddard - a true Blue.

This edition produced for the Book People Ltd,
Hall Wood Avenue, Haydock, St Helens WA11 9UL

First published in the UK by Scholastic Ltd, 2001

Text copyright © Terry Deary, 2001
Illustrations copyright © Martin Brown, 2001

ISBN 0 439 95436 3

CONTENTS

INTRODUCTION

History can be horrible because *people* can be horrible. Well, *most* people can be horrible *some* of the time … even you. And *some* people can be horrible *most* of the time … school bullies, school teachers and school children who pull the wings off flies.

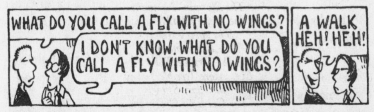

Then there are people who are *paid* to be horrible and torture innocent humans … tax collectors, traffic wardens and school dinner ladies…

And soldiers. Soldiers can be horrible because it's their job to kill their enemy – if they didn't the enemy would probably try to kill them. You can't go to war and behave like a gentleman, can you?

Some people in the past spent their whole lives fighting wars, so you can imagine how vicious they became. People like the Normans had to be really nasty.

The stormin' Normans were squidged into a corner of northern France and wanted to spread out – get more land. So they fought their way out. And it worked!

Some Normans, like William the Conqueror, hardly ever lost a battle. How did he do it? By being nastier than his enemies.

So you too can learn how to fight back with the help of a few lessons from the stormin' Normans. But be warned – you may become rich and successful, but you'll not be very popular. You will be remembered in history with hatred!

You have been warned!

TIMELINE

911 Charles the Simple, King of France, gives land in Northern France to the Viking Rollo and his people. Their nervous new neighbours call them 'North-men' ... that becomes 'nor-men' ... and finally Normans, geddit?

1017 The Normans set off to conquer the south of Italy. And the Italians have invited them! They've asked the Normans in to keep out some other invaders.

1047 William of Normandy, aged 19, wins his first great battle at Val-es-Dunes on the Norman border with France. Watch out for this teen terror.

1061 Normans begin their conquest of Sicily – but it will take them 30 years to complete because they are always outnumbered.

1066 William of Normandy defeats the English King Harold at the Battle of Hastings. He is crowned King of England and his Norman soldiers settle there.

1084 Germans attack Rome. Normans save the Pope and drive back the Germans – the Normans then raid Rome themselves. Well why not? They'd saved it for a rainy day.

1085 William the Conqueror orders the Domesday Book – a survey of everything everyone in England owns ... so he can have a share. (Today's government still does that.) A year later he dies and Norman William II takes the throne.

1095 Pope Urban II suggests that Christian knights should capture Jerusalem from the Muslims and give it to the Christian Church. Most of Europe agrees but the Normans lead the way. Great excuse to fight with God on their side.

1099 The Crusaders finally capture Jerusalem. With God on their side they massacre the Muslim men, women and children they find there.

1100 The Normans who remain in Jerusalem carve out a new Norman kingdom in the Middle East and call it their Holy Land. Meanwhile back in England William II is killed in a hunting accident ... or was it murder? Brother Henry I takes over.

1119 Henry I's only son dies in a shipwreck. There will be a long and nasty scrap to decide who gets his throne when he dies, which he does in...

1135 Henry I has chosen nephew Stephen to be the next king. Henry's

THIS IS MY FAVOURITE BOOK

WHAT'S IT ABOUT?

THINGS THAT ARE MINE

WE FIGHT FOR GOD!

WE DIE FOR NOTHING

OOPS

THERE'LL BE UTTER CHAOS IF YOU DROWN

SORRY

daughter, Empress Matilda, says, 'I'll fight you for the crown!' The wars bring almost 20 years of misery to England. These times are known as 'The Anarchy'.

1153 War ends when Stephen agrees that Matilda's son can have the throne when he dies. A year later Stephen keeps his promise – and dies. Peace at last.

1154 Henry II of England is from Anjou – an area in France to the south of Normandy. The Norman lords in England are no longer calling themselves Normans, but 'English'.

1199 Big Bad John becomes King of England and Duke of Normandy. But he isn't nicknamed 'Lack-land' for nothing…

1204 French King Philip II takes Normandy. The Normans in England have to choose – do they stay and become English? Or join the French to keep their Norman lands but lose their English ones? Most stay in England. The Normans become English or French but Norman no more.

BIG BAD BILL

Of all the Normans, William of Normandy (1028–1087) has to be the most famous, known to the world as William the Conqueror. Bill became Duke of Normandy at the age of 7 and had a scary childhood, always in danger of being murdered by people who wanted his land. He grew up tough enough not only to survive, but to be the first Norman to become a king when he conquered England.

Terrible teen

Bill's first major battle was in 1047, at Val-es-Dunes, at the age of just 19. Historian William of Poitiers said:

> *Young William was not scared at the sight of the enemy swords. He hurled himself at his enemies and terrified them with slaughter. Some of the enemy met their death on the field of battle, some were crushed and trampled in the rush to flee and many horsemen were drowned as they tried to cross the river Orne.*

SPLASH, GURGLE, PUSH, SHOVE, HACK, CHOP!

William later marched on the town of Alençon. The defenders barred its gates and then made fun of his mother's peasant family. They cried:

William was furious. When he eventually captured the town he took 32 of the leading citizens of Alençon and paraded them in front of the townsfolk. Then he had their hands and feet cut off.

Mrs Conqueror

William married Matilda in about 1052 or 1053. She was a tiny woman (about 127 cm), but tough, and proved to be a loyal and clever wife.

You have to sort the facts from the fiction about Matilda though! French historians told the following story…

William was visiting Count Baldwin V when he fell in love with his daughter, Matilda. He asked if he could marry the girl but Matilda herself refused. She sneered...

William secretly went to her house at night where he beat her and kicked her. As the mauled Matilda lay battered on her bed she changed her mind. She said ...

The story is probably not true. The Normans were trying to show that their women loved violent men – because that's what the men wanted to believe!

Bill's last battle

William was back in France, attacking the town of Mantes, when he had his last illness. He'd had the town burned to the ground and (one story says) his horse was frightened by the shower of sparks.

The horse stumbled, William slammed his stomach against the front of his saddle and burst his fat gut. He died five weeks later after suffering in agony. Before he died he handed his crown and sword to his son William Rufus. But the moment he died the Norman lords panicked. With the

Conqueror dead there could be rebellions in their lands. Orderic Vitalis, writing 50 years after the death, described what happened next…

As soon as William died, the richest of the Norman lords mounted their horses and hurried off to defend their castles. The servants – seeing that their masters had disappeared – laid their hands on the weapons, the gold and silver plate, the rich cloth and the royal furniture. The corpse of the king was left almost naked on the floor.

The disappearing conqueror

William's body was eventually taken to Caen to be buried in the cathedral William had founded. The journey to the church was interrupted by a fire in the town – they dropped the body, fought the fire, then carried on.

Later the funeral service was interrupted by a local man who said…

THE GROUND WHERE YOU'RE BURYING WILLIAM BELONGS TO ME! I WANT TO BE PAID BEFORE YOU PUT HIM IN THE GRAVE!

He was paid!

Then the clumsy undertakers tried to cram the fat body into a small stone coffin and bits fell off. The smell was so disgusting the bishop rushed through the burial service and everyone ran for it.

Rest in peace, William? No. Only until 1522. In that year the curious Catholic Church had the tomb opened to inspect the body.

Rest in peace, William? No. Only until 1562. In that year Protestants raided the church, broke open tombs and scattered skeletons. All that was left was Will's thigh bone. That was re-buried and a fine monument was built.

Rest in peace, William's thigh bone? No. Only until 1792 when the French Revolution mobs demolished his monument.

Rest in peace, William? For the moment. A simple stone slab now marks the spot where he was buried.

But what happened to that thigh bone? Some say the 1792 rioters threw it out – some say it's still there. Perhaps someone should open the tomb again and find out!

UNLIKELY LEGENDS

Historians have a tough time trying to sort out the truth. They may come across stories in old scripts, but those stories could be untrue.

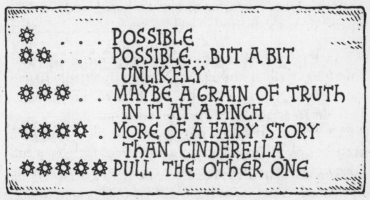

...then in 1075 I went to the moon with the Pope.

Here are a few tales from Norman days that may have some truth in them (one-star porkies) – or may be just legends (five-star whacking great fibs). What would you make of these tales?

✵ . . . . POSSIBLE
✵✵ . . . POSSIBLE...BUT A BIT UNLIKELY
✵✵✵ . . MAYBE A GRAIN OF TRUTH IN IT AT A PINCH
✵✵✵✵ . MORE OF A FAIRY STORY THAN CINDERELLA
✵✵✵✵✵ PULL THE OTHER ONE

Norman nonsense?

1 William the Conqueror's dad, Duke Robert, met his mum, Herleve, while she was dancing in the road. He fell in love with her. Of course this is quite possible – unlike today when dancing in a road would get you a) arrested or b) flattened by a flying Ford Fiesta. ✵✵ STARS

2 Before William the Conqueror was born his mother had a dream. She dreamed a tree was growing from her and the shade of the tree covered Normandy and England. (Just as

the son that would grow from her would cast his shadow over Normandy and England. Geddit?) Nowadays her doctor would tell her the bad dreams mean a) nothing or b) she's been eating toasted cheese sandwiches before going to bed.

✿✿✿✿✿ STARS

3 William the Conqueror was tormented by enemies who said he was just the son of a tanner's daughter – a tanner turns animal skins into leather. His grandfather, Fulbert, lived in Falaise where there were a lot of leather-makers, so it is possible. But another story says Fulbert had the charming job of preparing corpses for burial – tidying them up and dressing them.

I THINK YOU'LL LOOK FABULOUS IN THE BLUE TUNIC AND BROWN LEGGINGS

William would have liked that because a) it's a steady job and b) William could go out and kill enough people to keep Grandpa rushed off his feet! ✿ STAR

4 Rollo the Viking was offered the land of Normandy by Charles the Simple in 910. 'Let's make a deal,' Charles said (simply). 'You Vikings can simply have Normandy but I simply insist on being your king. You must simply do homage to me. To show you accept me as king you must simply kiss my foot.' Rollo didn't fancy that much ... would you? So he sent one of his soldiers to kiss Charlie's foot. The soldier didn't want to grovel so he grasped the king's foot and lifted

it up to his lips. Of course this tipped Charles the Simple's throne back and he was simply thrown to the ground.

Big laughs for Rollo who was probably a) rolling with laughter or b) Rollo-ing with laughter. ✿✿✿ STARS

5 William the Conqueror was just a teenage duke when he was visiting the castle of one of his lords. He was tipped off that the lord planned to kill him. William escaped from the castle in darkness, rode for 16 hours through the night and came to the wide estuary of the Vire river. He was able to cross it because the tide was out (very lucky) and reached the castle of a friend before he could be caught. He was lucky that a) his horse didn't stumble on dark, uneven roads and break two necks and six legs (William's AND the horse's, if you hadn't worked it out, dummy) or b) he didn't get stopped for speeding by policemen with radar guns. ✿✿ STARS

6 In 1064 Harold Godwinson of England was the man most likely to take the English throne when Edward the Confessor died (which he did in 1066). The story goes that Harold was crossing the English Channel when his ship was caught in a storm. Harold was recognized and taken to William of Normandy (who also fancied himself as King of England when old Ed kicked the bucket). Harold had to promise he would let William become king when Ed died. William set

him free … and Harold broke his promise in 1066. But is the story true? Would Harold *really* give away his kingdom?

This is a story told by Norman historians who want to show that a) Harold was a rotten cheat who broke his promises and b) William was the rightful king of England – he wasn't 'William the Conqueror' in 1066, he was 'William the I've-just-popped-over-the-Channel-to-take-what-is-rightfully-mine-old-chap'. ✿ STAR

Odd English

If the Normans had some strange beliefs, the English people had some stories that were even stranger!

1 In 1080 a man called Eadulf died in the village of Ravensworth in northern England. His relatives came to watch over the corpse but they were shocked when Eadulf sat up and said, 'Don't be afraid! I have risen from the dead. Make the sign of the cross on yourselves and on the house.' When they'd done that the house was filled with birds that flew in everyone's faces till a priest sprinkled them with holy water. Eadulf said, 'I've visited Hell, where I've seen the wicked tortured, and Heaven where I've seen a few old friends.' He also warned, 'I've seen places being prepared in Hell for some living people! One of them was Waltheof – English Earl of Northumberland.'

Shortly after this Waltheof became the only English leader to be executed by William the Conqueror. Weird? Or wacky?

✿✿✿✿✿ *STARS*

2 An English rebel, Edric the Wild, tried to make trouble for William the Conqueror in 1067. This Edric went out for a stroll after dinner one evening and came across a group of fairies dancing. Edric fell in love with one of these little ladies and married her. When Edric was defeated William the Conqueror ordered that this fairy wife should be brought to court so he could meet her. What on earth would big bullying Bill say to a fairy? 'Lend us your wand'?

✿✿✿✿✿ *STARS*

3 King Harold was slaughtered at the Battle of Hastings in 1066. But the English told a story that he survived the battle, buried under a pile of bodies. A peasant woman found him and nursed him back to health. He hid in a cellar in Winchester for two years before leading attacks on the hated Normans. In time he got religion and became Harold the hermit. Many English would love to believe their last great hero survived. Dream on. Just a little more possible than fairies. ✿✿✿✿ *STARS*

Painful poisoners

The Norman historians had a thing about poison! If someone died suddenly then they said, 'It could well have been poison!' Here are a few curious cases for you to judge, Sherlock…

1 William the Conqueror invited Count Conan of Brittany to join him in the conquest of England in 1066. Count Conan said:

NO! I WON'T GO BECAUSE YOU NORMANS POISONED MY FATHER TWENTY-SIX YEARS AGO!

The story goes that William decided to settle Conan and got one of Conan's lords to take the count's hunting horn and gloves. These were smeared with poison. When Count Conan went hunting he wiped his mouth with the poisoned glove and died. He was really out for the count!

COUNT DOWN

Was William really guilty of this murder? Possibly, though Conan died two months after the Normans landed at Hastings.

It's a lesson to us all: **a)** don't wipe your mouth on the back of your glove or **b)** get your teacher to taste your gloves before you put them on.

2 In 1060 Robert of Gere came to a nasty and suspicious end. Norman historian Orderic wrote…

> One day Robert was sitting happily by the fire and watched his wife holding four apples in her hand. He playfully snatched two from her and didn't realize that they were poisoned. He ate them though his wife told him not to. The poison took effect and after five days he died.

Again it's possible that he *was* poisoned.

And another lesson: a) do what your wife tells you or b) don't snatch food from someone else's hand ... especially if you don't know when they last washed that hand!

3 Lady Mabel of Belleme plotted to poison her husband's enemy, Arnold of Echauffour, who was visiting them. She placed a poisoned goblet of wine on the table and waited. Unfortunately her brother-in-law, Gilbert, came in sweaty and hot from hunting. He cried...

...snatched up the poisoned cup and swallowed the lot.

He died.

Now, if you'd been Mabel, you'd have given up, wouldn't you? Not her. She bribed one of enemy Arnold's servants to put poison in his food, which he did. Arnold died. Second time lucky!

A lesson there: **a)** if at first you don't succeed, try again or **b)** don't take wine from Mabel's table (or read the label if you're able).

4 Lady Mabel then survived a poison plot against herself. The monks of Saint Evroul were fed up with her visiting them with dozens of servants to eat all their best food.

She returned, and ate … and fell ill. She ordered that her baby be brought to her for feeding. She let the baby suck milk at her breasts. The baby died. (From poison in his mother's body?)

And Mabel? She survived.

A lesson for us all: **a)** don't go where you're not wanted and **b)** don't have a murdering meanie like Mabel for a mother!

5 William the Conqueror's dad (Robert) became Duke of Normandy only after his older brother (Richard) died suddenly. Many people believed that William's dad had poisoned his uncle in order to get his hands on Normandy.

If Robert was poisoned a few years later (and some say he was) then he must have died thinking...

The lesson seems to be: *never* trust *any* Norman who offers you food or drink!

Of course Norman cooks weren't too fussy about washing their hands after using the toilet or picking their scabs or patting a dog. They didn't know about germs and hygiene. A lot of people in those days must have died from germs in their food that gave them food poisoning.

1066 AND ALL THIS

1066 was a funny old year. It saw three kings in England and three great battles. And if the year 1066 had kept its own diary[1] it would have been packed with horrible history...

> **1 January**
> Happy New Year, everyone in England! Edward the Confessor is King of England. But he's a poorly man. Old Ed has no children and no one's very sure about who'll get the throne when he dies. There are a lot of English people who are nervous about the coming year. Harold Godwinson for one – he is the most powerful lord in England. He practically rules the south for Edward the Confessor while his brother, Tostig Godwinson, rules the north.
>
> Harold is a tough nut. For years the Welsh had been a problem . . . until Edward the Confessor sent Harold off to sort them out in 1063. Here's what happened. . .

THE FIGHTING WAS VICIOUS. THE WELSH SENT HAROLD SEVERED HEADS TO SHOW THEY TOOK NO PRISONERS. HAROLD DIDN'T MIND PLAYING BY THOSE RULES.

A WELSH PRISONER? EXECUTE HIM.

THE WELSH WERE SO BATTERED THEY TURNED AGAINST THEIR OWN LEADER, GRUFFYDD, AND BEGGED HAROLD FOR PEACE. HE TOLD THEM...

YOU CAN HAVE PEACE WHEN YOU BRING ME THE HEAD OF GRUFFYDD.

1. To be honest there is a diary that was kept by monks called *The Anglo-Saxon Chronicle* but it's got lots of boring bits.

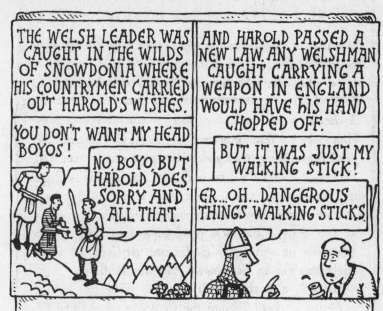

So Harold is a great warrior and the English army is in pretty good shape. I've a feeling it will need to be.

5 January
Edward the Confessor died. (I told you he was poorly, didn't I? You don't get much more poorly than that!)

6 January
Edward was buried today. That's a bit quick! His body can hardly be cold! And Harold Godwinson is crowned king. He didn't hang around did he? It will all end in tears, you mark my words.

February
That William of Normandy is upset! He's sent some of his

lords over to England with a message for King Harold. The message says. . .

1 Two years ago you promised that I would be King of England when Edward the Confessor died.

2 We also agreed that your sister would marry my son, while you married my sister.

Harold's reply is brief and to the point. . .

Dear William,

Edward the Confessor left the throne of England to me on his deathbed. We must respect the wishes of a dying man.

As for exchanging sisters I regret that I am now married to Ealdgyth. And I regret even more that my sister cannot marry your son since she has died. Perhaps you'd like me to send her corpse across to Normandy?

Harold (King of England)

I have heard that William has started building two thousand ships to invade England. There'll be trouble now!

24 April

Amazing! Fantastic and spooky! A comet has appeared in the skies over England! It's like a brilliant star with a tail. We all know it's a sign of a great disaster. The trouble is no one knows who will suffer the disaster – the English or the Normans. The English lords are telling Harold he should invade Normandy and put a stop to Wicked William's plans, but he won't do it.

> WHEN WILLIAM SETS SAIL
> WE'LL JUST SINK HIS SHIPS.
> WE'VE A STRONG NAVY. EASY.

May

Would you believe it? An invasion on the south coast and the navy was away in the north!! Were the invaders sent by that William of Normandy? No, they were led by Harold's own brother . . . treacherous Tostig. As soon as Harold marched from London to fight him, Tostig jumped in his boat and sailed away. They reckon he's doing a deal with the Viking they call Hardrada – Hard Ruler – for the two of them to attack the north of England. Poor Harold won't know if he's coming or going! But he will know who his friends are, and they don't include Wicked William, Horrible Hardrada or Terrible Tostig!

August

Still no sign of those Normans. Some say they're waiting for the right wind to carry their ships over the Channel.

8 September

Oh dear! Oh dear! Oh dear! Harold's army couldn't wait on the south coast for ever. They've had to go home to help with the harvest. But the navy's been sent to London and some terrible storms have wrecked a lot of them. I hope that Wicked William doesn't decide to come now!

They say William has lost a lot of ships in the same storms. Norman bodies were washed ashore and he had them buried secretly so the rest of the troops wouldn't be upset. Wimps. They'll never beat Heroic Harold even if they do get across the Channel!

20 September

Hardrada is here! He landed in Yorkshire and drew first blood. When I say blood I mean blood! Our Harold wasn't there so Hardrada attacked his earls. The English were driven into the marshes at Fulford near York and slaughtered. There were so many bodies the Vikings were able to cross the marsh by stepping on corpses like stepping-stones!

Now Horrible Hardrada wants food and drink from the people of York. He makes a terrible demand. . .

TO THE PEOPLE OF YORK,

WE WANT BREAD AND WE WANT WINE. SO THAT YOU DON'T BETRAY US I WANT 150 CHILDREN FROM YORK AS MY PRISONERS. MY MEN WILL COLLECT THEM FROM STAMFORD BRIDGE THIS MONDAY 25th. BE THERE OR BEWARE!

HARDRADA

25 September

What a day! Hardrada and Tostig turned up to collect their hostages at Stamford Bridge. But they had less than half of their army and they didn't have all their weapons! Guess who turned up to spoil their party? Our heroic Harold!

Harold made an offer to his brother Tostig.

TOSTIG, I OFFER YOU A THIRD OF THE KINGDOM IF YOU WILL GIVE IN.

WHAT ABOUT MY ALLY, HARDRADA?

I OFFER HIM JUST 7 FEET ...ENOUGH TO BURY HIM!

I DIDN'T BRING THE KING OF NORWAY TO ENGLAND TO BETRAY HIM. WE WILL FIGHT YOU, HAROLD.

And what a fight it was! A Viking hero blocked the bridge and slew 40 English before they could cross. The English sent a boat under the bridge, pushed a pike through the planks and stabbed him from below.

Harold's men swarmed over the Vikings. Hardrada, with little armour on, took an arrow in the windpipe and died. Tostig was hacked down when he refused to surrender.

Harold's English have defeated the invaders. The man is unbeatable! Now he is heading south just in case Wicked William lands there. He leaves his exhausted northern army behind. He'll have fresh men from the south if he needs them.

28 September

It's all happening this week! William the Norman has landed with his army on the south coast as Harold rides to meet him. That Wicked William was soon spreading stories about Harold. . .

DID YOU KNOW YOUR EVIL HAROLD KILLED HIS BROTHER TOSTIG AND SLICED ThE HEAD OFF THE CORPSE?

14 October

Gallant Harold finally came face to face with Duke William today near Hastings. And that's where Harold will be staying. The English fought all day but in the end the Norman knights and archers destroyed them. They say Harold was wounded in the eye and cut to pieces by William's knights. There is even a story that Wicked William himself had a chop or two at the corpse. Harold's brothers died with him. So mark today in your calendars for all time. It's the end of Saxon England and the start of Norman England.

15 October

King Harold's corpse has been taken to the seashore and buried under a pile of stones. The cruel conqueror William refused to give him a Christian burial. But he did give him a headstone reading:

HAROLD, YOU REST HERE, TO GUARD THE SEA AND SHORE

October

William and the Normans have been taking town after town as they march to London. The English have no castles to make it harder for William. But William and his Normans were almost stopped by something they got from Canterbury . . . the disease of dysentery. William and his soldiers are starting to fall sick with vomiting, fever and diarrhoea with blood. Some die but William lives.

November

London has surrendered and begs William to take the crown.

25 December

It's 'Happy Christmas, Your Grace,' as Duke William was crowned King of England. The cheers of his Normans inside Westminster Abbey made the soldiers outside think there was a riot. They started burning and looting the city. William was crowned amidst flames! Still, this is what we'll have to expect now the Normans are in charge.

31 December

Goodbye from 1066. And many happy New Years to you all. You'll forget many things in your lifetime, but you'll never forget heroic Harold, William the Conqueror or me . . . 1066.

LIVE LIKE A NORMAN

Name that Norman

The Normans' Viking ancestors often gave their people nicknames but they didn't always call people the nicknames to their face. Harold Bluetooth may not have minded you using his nickname too much. But you'd probably have got a clout from Olaf the Stout!

The Normans carried on this habit with some of their leaders. Duke William's mother wasn't married to his father so his enemies called him William the Bastard … his friends (and sensible people) called him William the Conqueror.

Can you match the nicknames to these Normans?

Of course the meanest-sounding nickname went to the French king who invited the Vikings into Normandy in the first place – he was Charles the Simple. But in those days 'simple' meant 'pure' rather than stupid. Simple, isn't it?

Eat like a Norman

The Norman recipes we have are not very detailed. If you want to taste Norman-type food then you have to work a lot of it out for yourself – how much to put in each mixture and how long to cook it.

DO YOU THINK MY CAKE HAS BEEN IN LONG ENOUGH, MUM?

Here's a Norman dish you may like to try. It was probably eaten by the rich Normans and not their poor peasant farmers. If it doesn't work very well then have a cat or dog handy to help you eat it.

Nasty Norman pasty

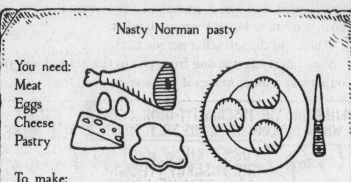

You need:
Meat
Eggs
Cheese
Pastry

To make:
Boil the meat in a pan of water till it is cooked.
Make pastry and roll it out.
Chop up the cooked meat, beat the eggs and grate the cheese then stir them together.
Make the mixture into balls about the size of apples.
Wrap each ball in pastry.
Bake in a hot oven till the pastry is golden brown.

To serve:
Place on a wooden plate and eat with a knife and fingers.

Remember to get an adult to do the sharp knife bits and the boiling water stuff. It is much more fun to watch an adult chop their scalded fingers off than it is to chop your own. After all, you probably need your fingers to pick your nose, don't you?

It shouldn't kill you ... though it is best to remember: the Normans ate this and they are all dead!

Salty science
Of course your meal will taste better with salt in it. In Norman times you couldn't pop along to the local

supermarket and buy a packet. To get some in your salt cellar you had to buy it from a salt seller.

Where did the salt seller get his salt?

Sometimes salt was dug from pits in the ground and you could make a lot of money if you owned a salt mine ...

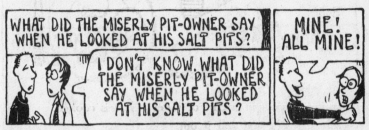

WHAT DID THE MISERLY PIT-OWNER SAY WHEN HE LOOKED AT HIS SALT PITS?

I DON'T KNOW. WHAT DID THE MISERLY PIT-OWNER SAY WHEN HE LOOKED AT HIS SALT PITS?

MINE! ALL MINE!

But if you lived close to the coast and wanted to save some money then you could make your own salt from sea water. The Normans knew enough science to be able to do it.

POOR WOMAN'S WEEKLY

Salt that supper

Want to give your family a real treat tonight? Then sprinkle their food with salt, fresh from the sea! Simply fill a pot with sea water and set it to boil. When the water's boiled away the salt will have formed a white crust around the pot. Wait till it cools – you don't want to burn those lovely hands, do you? Then scrape the salt from the sides of the pot and store it in a cool dry place till you need it. Scrummy!

Horrible Histories Health Warning: Don't try this at home. Sea water in the 2000s isn't as pure as it was in the 1000s!

As well as flavouring food, salt could be used to preserve it. In the days before fridges meat could be covered in salt to stop it going bad.

This was useful in the Norman world. There wasn't usually enough grass to keep all the animals over the winter. So any spare animals were killed and the meat salted. Would you enjoy the job of deciding which of those sweet little calves and lambs and piglets should feel father's axe?

Dazzling dressers

Peacocks have the fancy feathers and the terrific tails. Peahens look boring alongside them. And it was a bit like that in Norman times. It was the rich men who were the flashy dressers.

Peculiar 'poulaines'

Norman soldiers probably invented 'poulaines' – the famous shoes that had long, pointed toes. In time the toes curled up in great loops and had to be chained to the knee to stop the flop.

But in Norman times there was a story that the shoes were invented by Fulk, Duke of Anjou. (Anjou is just a bit to the south of Normandy.) The story goes that Fulk had a lump growing on his foot and he designed the shoes to hide the fact he had an ugly foot. It's possible that Fulk did wear the shoes but he probably didn't 'invent' them – he just borrowed the idea from his knightly Norman neighbours.

WARNING: Do not read the following if you are easily shocked or need a sense of humour transplant. Two hundred and fifty years after Fulk invented (or didn't invent) 'poulaines' they were turned into something quite disgraceful by some Frenchmen. They stuffed the long toes with sawdust and shaped them to look like a man's naughty bits. The French king Charles V banned such rude shoes in 1367.

True or false

History can be horribly difficult. Even a history teacher would struggle to get ten out of ten with these quick but quirky questions. Try these on some sad teacher, get them to answer true or false, and see who will be the conqueror…

1 A Norman boy could became a monk at the age of seven and would never be able to give up the monastery.

2 The Normans ate canaries on toast.

3 The Domesday Book wasn't called the Domesday Book.

4 Some Norman women used the poisonous deadly nightshade plant to make their eyes more attractive.

5 Norman minstrels played bagpipes.

6 Norman town houses had kitchens next to the dining room so the food stayed hot.

7 A Norman knight slept better in his tent if he had a dolly over his head.

8 The Normans enjoyed Easter eggs.

9 The Normans always built their castles on waste land so no one lost fields or houses.

10 Normans on the coast had a lifeboat rescue service for ships in the English Channel.

Answers:

1 False. Before the Normans invaded England it had been true that boys took vows at the age of seven that could never be broken. If they did leave the monastery then they became outlaws. But the Normans changed this. Boys spent nine years in the monastery and, at the end of that time, they could leave – or stay for ever. But there was a catch in some monasteries. If you left before the age of 16 you might have to pay the monks for what they had taught you! Imagine that! Having to pay to leave school!

LEAVE WHEN YOU'RE *NINE* ?? I THOUGHT IT WAS NINETY!

2 False. The Normans brought canaries from the Canary Islands (believe it or not). The Canary Islanders loved to eat the little feathered foodstuff but the Normans wanted them for their singing.

3 True. A hundred years after it was written the book was nicknamed the 'Domesday Book' because it was like the Christian Day of Judgement (Doomsday) in that there could be no appeal against it. You were stuck with what the book said about your land and your wealth. The book called itself a 'descriptio' which is a Latin word meaning a 'writing down'. It was kept in the Royal Treasury at Winchester and the early Normans knew it as 'The Winchester Book'. (No prizes for guessing why.) By 1170 people were calling it 'Domesday' and as late as the 1900s it was still being used to settle arguments over who owned what. Bet your school exercise books don't last that long!

4 True. But very rarely! Norman women in Western Europe used hardly any make-up. Rich women in Eastern Europe used lip colour and drops of deadly nightshade to make the black centre of the eyes (the pupils) open wide. Gorgeous.

5 True. The Normans enjoyed good music (which makes you wonder why they liked the bagpipes). With harps, fiddles, flutes, cymbals, bassoons, trombones and trumpets they could have tortured your eardrums till they burst.

6 False. The houses were made of wood and the roofs were thatched with reeds. If they caught fire the house could be destroyed in half an hour. Kitchens were built separately from the house so there was less chance of careless cooks setting the house on fire. Food would not be so hot when it reached the table. Better a cool dinner than a hot house, they reckoned.

7 True. The tent pole went through a hole in the roof – called an 'onion'! To stop the rain coming through the gap between pole and hole a cap was put on top. This cap was called a 'dolly'.

8 True. During Lent (the weeks before Easter) the Church did not allow Christians to eat eggs. So housewives would save up all their eggs to have as a special treat on Easter Day. They would be boiled and coloured with natural dye – try boiling an egg with onion skins and see what happens! Have your boiled eggs blessed by a priest and scoff them. Sorry – no chocolate eggs, fat face.

9 False. The Normans sometimes found new sites for their castles but they often built them slap bang in the middle of a town. And what do you usually have in the middle of a town? That's right, houses. What happened to the houses? The people were thrown out and they were flattened – 160 homes in Lincoln and another hundred in Norwich, for example. Eudo Dapifer built a castle at Eaton Socon over a church and graveyard. Spooky, eh?

10 False. Quite the opposite! In 1046 a fleet from Flanders was storm-damaged in the English Channel. People from the Norman coast villages hurried to the beaches and waved lanterns to guide the ships to the shore. When the storm-bashed sailors landed the villainous villagers massacred them and stole the cargoes from the ships!

TERRIFIC TALES

People in Norman times worked hard from sunrise to sunset – then they stopped because it was too dark to carry on. They were just like you after a hard day at school – they wanted some entertainment.

You turn on the television or the computer or even pick up a book. The Normans had none of these things. What they had were 'jongleurs'. A jongleur was a musician, a juggler, and an acrobat. He was also a story-teller. He recited or sang long story-poems about great heroes like Roland and Oliver.

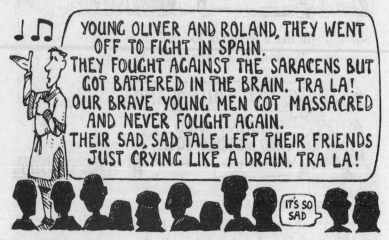

Oliver and Roland had been Christian knights and may really have existed. They fought a gallant but hopeless battle against the Saracens (the Norman name for Muslim warriors). The two friends faced a mighty army alone but Roland was too proud to call for help. They were killed, of course. The story was told as an example to Norman crusaders who were urged to copy their bravery.

There is a legend (it may even be true) that a jongleur led William the Conqueror's troops into the Battle of Hastings.

The Norman historian, Wace, said...

A minstrel named Taillefer went in front of the Norman army, singing and juggling with his sword while the troops marched behind singing the Song of Roland.

THEY MUST BE TOUGH IF THEY CAN PUT UP WITH THAT!

Sounds a bit like a bunch of football supporters on their way to a match. We don't know what Harold's English troops sang.

WE LOVE YOU ROLAND, WE DO!

ROLAND DIED AND SO WILL YOU!

Brave Brit 1

When the Normans arrived in England they found the British had their own legends – dead and living. The dead hero was King Arthur. The Normans loved the story of Arthur and their writers and poets turned him from a British warrior into a magical king. Here's how the story grew...

- In 1135 Geoffrey of Monmouth writes about Arthur. (Though another writer at that time says, 'It is quite clear that everything Geoffrey wrote about Arthur was made up.')
- In 1155 a jongleur called Wace tells Arthur's story and added a bit about a Round Table.

- In 1160 Chretien de Troyes adds bits to the story to make Arthur a knight in armour, not just a British warrior.
- In 1190 a poet called Robert be Boron adds the bit about Arthur's knights and the Holy Grail – the cup that Jesus drank from at the last supper. People who drink from that can live for ever.
- Around 1200-ish an English priest adds that Arthur isn't dead, just sleeping. He'll wake up when England is threatened again. (So where was the sleepy old wrinkly when William the Conqueror landed?)

But there's an even stranger story about the discovery of Arthur's tomb at Glastonbury Abbey.

Arthur's grave

In 1184 there was a disaster when Glastonbury Abbey burned down. The monks were poor and were desperate for money. They needed visitors. Tourists! Pilgrims! But how could they attract them?

There was one thing that might help…

BACK IN 1130 A WRITER MENTIONED THAT ARTHUR HAD VISITED GLASTONBURY ABBEY

SO? HOW DOES THAT HELP US?

Do you know? How could they cash in on that story and make Glastonbury a tourist attraction? Someone had a brilliant idea!

WHAT IF WE COULD PROVE THAT ARTHUR IS BURIED HERE?

BUT HE ISN'T!

NOT YET!

And, would you believe it, when the monastery was being rebuilt Arthur's tomb *was* found there! The monks' story was a good one. They said…

YEARS AGO AN OLD MONK WENT TO THE ABBOT AND HE BEGGED, 'PLEASE, ABBOT, WHEN I DIE I WISH TO BE BURIED IN THE ABBEY AT THE PLACE WHERE THE TWO PATHS CROSS.'

IN 1191 THE OLD MONK DIED AND WE BEGAN TO DIG AT THE PLACE HE HAD CHOSEN

BUT AS WE DUG WE CAME ACROSS THE COFFIN OF A WOMAN WITH HER HAIR STILL ATTACHED. THAT WOULD BE QUEEN GUINEVERE!

BELOW IT WE FOUND A COFFIN WITH A LEAD CROSS FIXED TO IT WITH ARTHUR'S NAME ON IT. THE BONES INSIDE THIS COFFIN WERE THOSE OF A VERY LARGE MAN. ARTHUR HIMSELF!

AND HERE'S THE LEAD CROSS TO PROVE IT!

Visitors and pilgrims flocked to the Abbey (even the King came to see the grave) and Glastonbury Abbey became the richest monastery in Britain.

But were the monks telling the truth? If you want to make a fortune then find a dead hero in your back garden. After 800 years some people still believe the story of Arthur's burial at Glastonbury! They even believe in his Round Table.

Do you believe it? Or is it just Norman nonsense?

Brave Brit 2

The living legend was the English freedom-fighter, Hereward the Wake. The truth is…

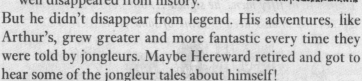

- Hereward went on fighting against William the Conqueror's forces when other English leaders had given up.
- Hereward joined forces with Danish invaders and robbed Peterborough Abbey to stop its riches falling into the hands of the Normans.
- The rebels hid in the marshes where the Normans eventually surrounded and captured them.
- Hereward escaped … and pretty well disappeared from history.

But he didn't disappear from legend. His adventures, like Arthur's, grew greater and more fantastic every time they were told by jongleurs. Maybe Hereward retired and got to hear some of the jongleur tales about himself!

Maybe Hereward's legendary deeds need a new jongleur epic for reciting around the fire at your castle hearth (or your nearest central-heating radiator will do if you don't live in a castle).

Hereward's revenge

My friends I'll sing a song to you, if you your seats will take;
I'll tell you all of our great hero, Hereward the Wake.
He was away from England when the Normans came to Hastings.
And missed the mighty battle where old Harold took a pasting.

Our hero came back home and found his younger brother dead.
'The dirty rotten Normans, they have killed our kid!' he said.
'I'll be revenged, you wait and see, with English help and Dane!'
And off he set to find some ways to bring the Normans pain.

When he arrived at his old house the great hall it was swarmin'
With knights and soldiers all around, each one a deadly
*   Norman.*
'I can't fight fifty men,' he sighed … our hero was not thick.
'To take them on I need to think of some real clever trick!'

Our Hereward decided as a Norman he would pose,
He pinched a pointy helmet (with that straight bit down the nose).

And then he slipped inside his home where Norman soldiers feasted.
He drank pure English water while the Normans wined and eated.

The bloated Normans fell asleep but Hereward was awake,
He took his knife and slit their throats, 'Take that!' he cried,
  'That take!'
Then Hereward he cut the Norman heads off at the neck.
'I'll teach you Norman nasties to go killing us, by heck!'

Then he found some nails and a hammer (in his garden shed),
And he decorated each doorway with a nasty Norman head.
So no one would come asking him, 'Now whose dead heads are
  those?'
He left their pointy helmets on (with that straight bit down the
  nose).

Some say the Normans caught our hero Hereward the Wake,
One day when he was fast asleep, and his brave life they taked.
But I am sure he still lives on, our Hereward the Wake,
Who found that fighting Norman knights was just a piece of cake.

TRA-LA! TRA-LA! OH FOL-DE-ROL! TRA-LA! TRA-LA! TRA-LEE! TRA-LA! TRA-LA! OH FOL-DE-ROL! I'LL BID YOU ALL GOOD-BYE-EE!

Did you know… ?

Hereward was given the name 'The Wake' because he was always 'watchful'. It didn't mean he was always awake.

He *did* go to sleep but he never slept in a bed! He always slept alongside it. An enemy could have sneaked in while Hereward the Wake wasn't awake. If the enemy attacked the bed then he'd miss Hereward the Wake who'd wake.

Good tip, that, for those of you who go away on school trips.

The knight visitor

Jongleurs had to be paid for their entertaining. They could choose to travel around … then they could sing the same songs over and over again, but they weren't sure when they'd get their next pay-day. The alternative was to stay in one castle … then they became known as minstrels and had to keep coming up with new songs all the time, but at least they were sure of food and shelter.

Generally poor people couldn't afford to hire a jongleur and they didn't have musical instruments themselves. So what could they do to entertain themselves and the kids? Tell stories, of course. Here is a story from Norman times that was told all over Europe. Are you sitting comfortably?

Once upon a time there was a brave young knight called Prince Hugo. There was nothing our young Hugo liked better than doing a bit of embroidery. Hugo made all his own dresses and let his hair grow down to his waist.

'He's a bit ... odd,' the courtiers in his castle whispered to one another. But Hugo had his reasons. He didn't let the gossip needle him.

Hugo could have passed for a girl ... which, as it happened, was exactly what he wanted.

You see, he'd heard about the poor princess Hilde. She was the most beautiful, clever and tragic princess in the whole of Normandy ... maybe even in the whole world. Hilde's father, Count Walgund, had locked her in a tall tower. The tower was in a forest and the forest was infested with the wildest wolves in the west.

Count Walgund was so devoted to his dear daughter that he didn't want to lose his lovely lass to some layabout lout of a lad. He didn't want her running off and getting married – unless it was to a perfect husband.

One day Hugo put on his best frock, embroidered by himself with a squillion sequins he'd sewn on, and arrived at Count Walgund's castle. 'I am a lost lady whose homeland has been conquered by a cruel king. I ask only a bed for the night, good count!'

Before the count could answer, his countess cried, 'Look at that dress! What a work of a needle-woman's wondrous art! You simply must teach our daughter how to embroider like that, mustn't she, Count?'

To say the dress was the work of a woman is, of course, sexist. Countess Walgund wouldn't get away with it today, would she lads? Boys today know their needles from their nine-pound notes, oh dear me, yes! Anyway the daft old bat was wrong because Hugo was a bloke!

Now we know that's exactly what our clever little Hugo was after all the time, don't we? Next day he was in the tower and teaching the lovely Hilde the ropes ... well the threads, if you know what I mean.

Hilde loved her new chum – loved her deep voice, her strong hands, her broad shoulders. 'Excuse me,' Hilde said after a week. 'But would I be correct in thinking that you are really a man disguised as a woman.'

Hugo clicked his long fingers. 'Curses! How did you guess?'

'I think it's probably the beard that gave you away,' Hilde confessed.

Hugo rubbed his rough chin and sighed. 'Sorry. You don't mind, do you?'

'Mind!' Hilde cried. 'I'm chuffed to fluffy fairy feathers! I think you're gorgeous!'

'You're not so bad yourself,' Hugo admitted.

Before another week was out they were married. Then Hugo declared, 'I have to leave now. I must find a way to persuade your father that I will make him a good son-in-law.'

'That's a bit sudden, my pet!' Hilde moaned, but she saw the sense in what he said. Hugo chopped his hair, and swapped his female dress for male chain-mail. Off he rode on a crusade where he fought side-by-side with Count Walgund. They were gone a long time. A long, long time ... well, a couple of years anyway ... and things had been happening in the tall tower.

'Come home with me, my brave young friend,' Count Walgund said to Hugo. Now, we know that's exactly what our clever little Hugo was after all the time, don't we?

But as they rode close to the tall tower Walgund saw a wolf cross the path and cried, 'After it! Kill it! We can't have wolves wandering my paths and putting my people in peril!'

So they chased the wolf who turned to face the fierce knights. The wolf dropped a bundle she was carrying and slipped off into the deep dark trees. But the knights saw the white linen bundle wriggling. They stopped and picked it up. It was a baby boy!

'Good grief! Wonder who you belong to, my little man!' Walgund warbled. 'What a wonderful child. Wouldn't mind one like that for my grandson! Let's visit my daughter in a nearby tower. See if she can care for it till we find the rightful mother.'

When they reached the tower and unlocked the door Hilde rushed out.

Was she going to fuss over her father?

Was she going to hug Hugo?

No!

She ran across the courtyard and snatched the baby from the two men and wailed, 'My baby! The washerwoman left the kitchen door open this morning and he crawled off into the forest! I was sure he'd be killed by wolves!'

'Your baby?' Count Walgund said in wonder. 'Who's the father?'

Hilde raised her arm and pointed at Prince Hugo. 'Why, Hugo here!'

The count was confused, you can count on that. But, when he finally understood he happily hugged his daughter, his grandson and his son-in-law.

'What a day!' Hugo sighed. 'I've gained a son I never knew I had.'

53

'What a day!' Walgund cried. 'I've gained a son and a grandson I never knew I had!'

'I've waited for your return before I named the child,' Hilde said. 'What should we call him?'

Walgund looked at Hugo. Hugo looked at Walgund. The two knights looked at one another. They nodded. They said it together. 'Wolf, of course'.

Hilde and Hugo lived happy hever hafter.

NORMAN WISDOM

Are you as wise as a Norman? To understand the past you have to know how the people *thought*. Here are a few Norman beliefs...

1 *The Normans believed*... that many of their Muslim enemies were cowards. The Normans had won great victories in Europe where their charging knights smashed the enemy to the ground. But when the Norman Crusaders met the Muslim forces they had problems. The Muslims didn't line up and wait to be smashed to the ground! Instead they rode in a circle around the Crusaders and shot arrows at them from a distance.

WHY CAN'T THEY STAND STILL AND BE KILLED LIKE EVERYONE ELSE?

URK

Many Norman knights believed there was a reason for this...

THE MUSLIMS HAVE MORE BLOOD IN THEIR BODIES THAN WE HAVE. THEY ARE AFRAID OF GETTING HURT BECAUSE THEIR BLOOD WILL BURST OUT

Normans later learned to respect their Muslim enemies.

2 *The Normans believed*... that living too long in the Holy Land – what we call the Middle East today – was unhealthy. The hot climate and the strong wine affected the brain. (Of

course the easy answer would be not to drink the wine, but the water could be even more deadly ... and Coca-Cola hadn't been invented.) As a result people back in Europe said...

THE WEATHER OUT THERE MAKES PEOPLE MAD THEN DEAD!

3 *The Normans believed*... that painful punishments were the fairest. If they locked a criminal in jail then the family might starve. That would punish the innocent family. So, instead, they thought it was better to make a public display of the criminal – parade them in the stocks so that everybody could see this was a person not to be trusted. For more serious crimes they could decide to cut a bit off a criminal – a hand or a nose, perhaps. The criminal could then go back to work and support the family!

BUT I'M A HANDY MAN!

4 *The Normans believed*... that God would help them to give justice to criminals. Like the English before them they settled some cases by having a trial by 'ordeal'. A woman accused of theft could be made to hold a red-hot iron bar. Her hand was bandaged. If it healed she was innocent. A man could be tied up and thrown into water that had been blessed – if he sank he was innocent. (A bit like witch trials of later years.)

5 *The Normans believed...* that God was on their side, especially when they were fighting against the Muslims in Sicily or the Holy Land. The head of the Catholic Church, the Pope, told them, 'Look, lads, it's OK to kill those Muslims. God will forgive you.' So the Norman knights hacked away happily, believing it wasn't murder ... even when it was. It wasn't only the Pope who said killing was all right. God sent a messenger from heaven personally! None other than Saint George! At the battle of Cerami in 1063 he turned up to help 130 Normans defeat thousands of Muslims. The soldiers reported...

> SAINT GEORGE APPEARED ON A WHITE HORSE WITH A LANCE. THERE WAS A FLAG ON THE END OF THE LANCE WITH A WONDERFUL CROSS ON IT. WE'D HAVE LOST IF HE HADN'T LED OUR CHARGES!

The Pope believed the story and sent a flag, like the one in the vision, for the Normans to carry into future battles.

Saint George turned up again 35 years later at the battle for Antioch in the Holy Land. An unknown writer said…

> *Our soldiers saw a countless army of men on white horses whose banners were all white. When our men saw this they realized this was help sent by Christ and the leader was Saint George. This is quite true for many of our men saw it.*

ALL WHITE?

YES, THANK YOU

Sadly old Georgie wasn't around at Hattin in 1187 when the Crusaders were smashed. Perhaps it was his day off! He then returned a few years later to help Richard the Lionheart win another victory in the Holy Land. Bet the Crusaders wished he'd make his mind up … or send a letter to let them know he'd be around!

6 *The Normans believed*… that their doctors knew best. In the 1100s a knight was wounded in the leg and the wound became infected. An Arab doctor treated the wound and it started to get better.

THANKS, DOC!

عفوا!

it's nothing

An Arab soldier, Usamah Ibn Munqidh described what happened...

Yesterday a doctor arrived from Europe. A small man with a curling brown beard and rather dirty hands. 'What are you doing to this knight?' he demanded.

'I am placing a herbal plaster on the wound to help it heal,' the Arab doctor said.

'Herbal plaster! Nonsense!' the European doctor snorted. 'You Arabs are ignorant, simple people. You know as much about medicine as I do about the moon.' He turned to the knight and said, 'I have seen wounds like this many times. They fester and the leg turns green. The blood is poisoned and the poison kills the patient.'

The knight turned pale. 'Is there nothing you can do to stop this?'

'Only one thing,' the doctor from Europe told him. 'We must cut off the leg before it turns bad!'

'Cut off my leg! the knight moaned. 'I'll never ride or fight again!'

'You'll never ride or fight if you die from the poisoned blood. Make up your mind, man. Lose the leg or lose your life!'

'Then I must lose my leg,' the knight whispered.

The doctor called for a soldier to fetch an axe and he instructed the man where to strike the leg. The Arab doctor turned to me and said, 'This is madness! Can you do nothing to stop him?'

I shook my head. 'They are guests in our country. We must respect their customs.'

The knight turned on his side and I held his arms while the doctor stretched the leg out on a board of wood. When the axe came down the scream of the knight was terrible to hear. 'Again, man! Again!' the doctor from Europe cried, 'You failed to cut through!'

The second blow removed the leg. Blood from the wound soon stopped flowing. Blood does not flow long from corpses. The horror of the operation had killed the man.

The doctor from Europe shrugged his narrow shoulders. 'Ah, well. I had to try. He would have died anyway.' Then he left to practise his brutal skills on some other unlucky patients.

The Arab doctor turned to me and said, 'Such a waste.'

If I am ever wounded in battle then I hope my God lets me be treated by an Arab doctor and not a European butcher.

LITTLE VILLEINS

The Normans ran their countries under a 'feudal system'. Imagine that as a pyramid …

This is the king who sits at the top and owns the lot.

These are the barons who guard the king's land, and train the men to fight for the king who sits at the top and owns the lot.

These are the knights who look after the villages, and fight for their barons who guard the king's land, and train the men to fight for the king who sits at the top and owns the lot.

These are the villeins who work on the land and work for the knights who look after the villages, who fight for their barons who guard the king's land, and train the men to fight for the king who sits at the top and owns the lot.

These are the serfs who own no land but are owned by the knights who look after the villages, who fight for their barons who guard the king's land, and train the men to fight for the king who sits at the top and owns the lot while they own nothing, not even their bodies.

And lowest of all were the village children – nothing much changes there, then.

Tasks for tots

Was it pleasant being a peasant child? You'd have no school to go to! (So you couldn't learn to read and have the joy of *Horrible Histories* books, of course.)

What would you do all day with no school to imprison and torment you – no sick-making SATs, no dreadful detentions, no rotten reports, no evil essays and hideous homework! Would you be bored without these cool classroom capers?

Of course not! Your parents would find you work as soon as you could walk. Children in Norman times didn't have newspaper rounds and they probably didn't have to keep their bedrooms tidy or help with the washing up. Instead they helped on the land.

You'd have to...

- **collect wood** from the forest for the family fire (but watch out for the big bad wolves and outlaws). Every November villeins (and their children) gathered baskets full of wood for their lord's winter fires. For each basket they gathered he gave them one log!

THIS IS A LOG?

- **collect acorns** and beech nuts from the forest floor in autumn to feed the family pigs. (Then kill and eat the pig in winter and get your own back!)
- **prod the oxen** in the bum with a sharp stick so they'll pull the plough. (But be careful the angry ox doesn't turn and prod you in the bum with its horns.)

I THINK YOUR SHARP STICK IS A LITTLE TOO SHARP

- **turn the grindstone** at harvest time so the men can sharpen their sickles. (Such a boring job you'll be sickle of it in no time.)
- **polish the arrow heads** of your father's arrows using sand (and an arrow strip of cloth).

The good news is the Church banned work on a Sunday. So there's just the chance you may find time to play a game or two...

Games you may want to play

Bubble beaters

Children in Norman times enjoyed blowing bubbles just as children (and some sad grown-ups) do today. The Norman children didn't have plastic loops – they used hollow stalks of straw. Instead of washing-up liquid they'd use Norman bath soap, but it worked the same. If you want to check...

You need:
- a teaspoon of washing-up liquid stirred in half a cup of water
- drinking straws
- a watch with a second hand

To play:

Place one end of a straw in the mixture. Blow gently at the other end till a bubble appears. (Don't suck or you'll end up with the cleanest tonsils in town!)

With two or more players the winner is the one whose bubble lasts longest.

Conkering

William wasn't just a Conqueror. He was a conker-er too! The Normans taught the English the game of conkers. People still play it today – clever kids play conkers but so do adults who take it quite seriously and have a world championship every year! (They're bonkers.) If you care to try it then you will be playing a game about a thousand years old...

You need:
- at least one conker for each player
- string – cut to lengths about half a metre long
- a meat skewer

To make:
Drill a hole through the centre of the conker with the skewer. Push a piece of string through the hole. Tie a knot in the string so the conker can't slip off.

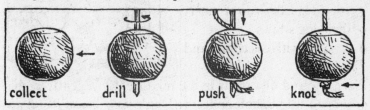

To play:
Toss a coin to decide who goes first. Player 1 swings their string to smash their conker into player 2's. If you hit the conker have another go. (If you miss you don't go again till it's your turn.) Player 2 then has a go at hitting player 1's conker. The first player to shatter the other's conker is the winner.

Punching puppets
Boys dressed in chain-mail coats, carried small lances and shields and played. We don't know what the rules were but

they probably charged at one another the way the grown-ups did on horses. (A point was scored every time a knight shattered his lance on his opponent's shield.) And no doubt there were accidents where smashing shields led to broken noses and splintered lances went into eyes. In other words, nothing too serious and only the odd death here and there.

A much safer game was fighting with puppets. If the weather was bad then the children got out their string puppets. These were about 30 to 40 cm high. The children stood (or knelt) facing one another and pulled the strings to make their puppets fight.

Super skating
In the 1100s William Fitz Stephen wrote about young men skating on the ponds and rivers in winter. If you want to go to your local ice-rink and save on the cost of hiring ice-skates then here's the way to do it ...

You need:
- the shin bones of a sheep or pig (from your local butcher – tell him it's for your poor pooch and he'll give them free!)
- strips of cloth (rip up your bedclothes or a teacher's shirt)
- two broom-handles
- a cushion

To make:

Boil the bones in a pot till the flesh drops off and the bones are white and clean. (Add carrots and onions to the water to make soup for when you get home chilled.)

Use strips of cloth to bind the bones to the bottom of your shoes and around your ankles.

Stuff the cushion down the back of your pants. (You'll look stupid but it will stop you getting a bruised and battered bum.)

Sharpen the bottom end of the broom handles and use them to push yourself along (like skis).

bones

boil

bind

bot

broom handles

To play:

Step on to the ice. Move one foot in front of the other and go as far as you can until you fall flat on your backside.

Don't ask why anyone would want to do it. People do this at ice rinks all over the country and get a strange twisted pleasure out of it. Some even try it without padding in their pants! Crazy.

Did you know…?

Normans also enjoyed sledging down hills in snowy weather. Instead of wooden sledges they used a large chunk of ice from a nearby pond. That's an ice way to save money.

Polo

Polo is the sport played on ponies where you try to hit the ball with a stick into a goal. It was invented in Persia around 600 BC and it was meant as a training exercise for horse soldiers. The Muslims were playing it when the Normans arrived in the Holy Land and the Crusaders copied it. Norman boys training to be knights would enjoy it. (Peasants like you and me couldn't afford the horses, of course.) There could be dozens on each side and it was more like war than a ball game.

In Persia the queen and her ladies played it but the Crusaders would never have allowed women to join in. (Probably for the same reason men don't like women to play in their football teams – the men are scared of getting beaten!)

To enjoy this ancient sport today, here's an easy way to do it indoors…

You need:
- a five-a-side football pitch
- hockey sticks
- a tennis ball

To play:
Divide into two equal teams of ten- (or twelve- or fifty-) a-side. Players ride piggy-back on their team-mates. (Switch over when the 'horse' gets tired.) The hockey sticks are used to hit the ball into the opponents' goal. (The sticks must *not* be used to trip opponents' horses, smack opponents in the mouth or to annoy teacher by rattling them up and down wall bars.)

Did you know… ?
In China (AD 910) one of the Emperor's favourite relatives was killed playing polo. Emperor A-pao-chi gave the order to have all of the surviving players beheaded.

Games you wouldn't want to play

Slinging scarecrows
Country children acted as killer scarecrows. They didn't just shoo the birds away – they killed the little blighters. Not only did a dead crow leave your parents' precious crops – it could also make a nice snack for dinner.

So learn the Scarecrow song from *The Wizard of Oz* ('If I Only Had a Brain') and get out there and frighten all feathered fiends. Here's how…

You need:
- a bootlace (leather is best)
- a piece of leather about 5 cm square
- a table-tennis ball

To make:
Make a hole at opposite corners of the leather and thread the lace through. Make a loop in one end of the lace and loop it over your forefinger.

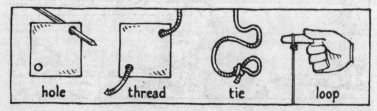

hole   thread   tie   loop

You now have a sling (similar to the one David used to kill Goliath, so be careful how you use it if you meet a giant!).

To shoot:

Place your ammunition (a table-tennis ball) in the leather pad. Hold the free end of the sling between your finger and thumb. Swing it quickly then release the free end of the lace. The ammunition will fly out.

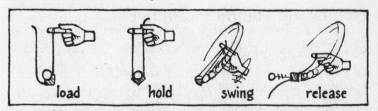

load   hold   swing   release

Note: It takes years of practice to get the action right, let alone hit a target! But don't worry, you have years sitting in freezing fields with nothing else to do. By the time you're grown up you'll be able to hit a tit at twenty paces!

Did you know... ?

Stone me, but it's true! The Norman army at the battle of Hastings is remembered for its archers. But the soldiers at the front were armed with slings. They'd have had a pocketful of stones but could always pick up more as they marched forward. Imagine getting one of those in your eye! Not a heroic way to go.

HE'S BEEN PEBBLE-DASHED!

The English fired back with stones attached to pieces of wood – a bit like a stone-age axe!

Scary school

From about the age of seven the sons of Norman lords and knights would train to be knights every afternoon. Good fun, eh? Riding and charging at targets (quintains) with your lance. Sword-fighting and murdering little rabbits and dear deer on hunting expeditions. Great fun!

Now the bad news. Your mornings would be spent in *lessons*. The castle clerks were there to keep the lords' records and keep their money right. But they also had the job of teaching you young knights your lessons.

These lessons were in lovely Latin! Yeuch!

And you don't need me to tell you what that means, do you? You do? Oh, very well. It means. 'Don't despair, have faith in God.' Write it on your next SATs paper and maybe God will give you a helping hand.

The Normans wrote their legal papers in Latin and (when you grew up) you'd have to put your seal on these so it helped if you knew what they meant.

And the really bad news… Each clerk-teacher was armed with a stout stick. No, this wasn't to help him point at the blackboard. It was to whack you across the shoulders if you weren't trying hard enough. And, as a tough little trainee knight you must never cry … or even show that it hurt you!

Chilling childhood

You think your life is hard, perhaps? Just be thankful you didn't grow up like one noble Norman boy. If you went through what he went through then you'd probably end up half crazed with fear. You certainly wouldn't sleep too well at night!

Here is his story…

I was just seven years old and starting to train as a knight when my father left home. He was the sixth Duke of Normandy and the only man who could keep the fighting lords from tearing it apart. The country was surrounded by our enemies. Everyone begged my father not to go but he said he wanted to go on a pilgrimage to Monte Gargano. (Some even said he went to beg God to forgive him for killing his own brother!) I never saw him

alive again. He died on his way back —
they say he may have been poisoned.

Before he left father got everyone to
agree that I should be the next duke. I
was left in the care of Count Alan but
he died suddenly.

Count Gilbert took his place — he
lasted a few months before he was
brutally murdered while he was out
riding. They told me Odo the Fat was
the killer.

My tutor Turold died soon after in
the same horrible way.

The head of my household was Osbern
and his death was the most hideous of all.
He was sleeping in my bed-chamber to
protect me from my enemies. I heard
the door open and saw William of
Montgomery slip in. His knife glinted in
the moonlight and before I could cry out
he had slit Osbern's throat.
Poor Osbern's blood lay in a
river over my floor.

Osbern's friends avenged him – they broke into William of Montgomery's house and slew the killer and everyone else they found there. Blood for blood.

My only true friend was my mother's brother, Walter. He slept in my room and if we heard any strange noises at night he would lead me to hide in the only place we felt safe – in the cottages of the poor.

Father, Count Alan, Count Gilbert, Turold and Osbern. All died so that others could control me and so control Normandy.

Brutal and dreadful days. Maybe that's where I learned that the only way to survive was to be violent. To strike anyone who threatened me. Maybe that's where I learned that the law of the Norman duke was simple ... kill or be killed.

Who was the child that had such a grim life before his ninth birthday? William, Duke of Normandy – later called William the Conqueror. Remember that childhood when you look at the ferocious man he grew to be.

MISERABLE MONARCHS

William the Conqueror was a pretty nasty Norman at times. But the Norman kings and queen who followed him could have their nasty moments too…

Red Bill

Name: William II (nicknamed 'Rufus') 1056–1100

Claim to fame: Rufus took over the throne of England from his dad, William the Conqueror. But the Conqueror gave Normandy to one of his other sons, Robert. Rufus went back to Normandy and spent half his time helping Robert to fight the French – and the other half trying to pinch Normandy from him!

Dreadful deeds: Rufus upset everybody and especially the men of the Church. He stole Church lands and Church money and refused to make the popular Anselm the new Archbishop of Canterbury. Then Rufus fell sick. 'You're dying!' the churchmen told him. 'Give us what you want or you will burn in Hell!' Rufus panicked, gave the churchmen what they wanted – then recovered!

DO YOU THINK I SHOULD HAVE TOLD HIM HE ONLY HAD A COLD?

Dire death: Rufus went hunting in the New Forest. He fired an arrow at a stag and missed. He then called to a knight, Walter Tirel, 'Shoot!' So Walter shot him ... the king, not the stag. Rufus was so unpopular no one blamed Tirel!

YOU KILLED THE KING, YOU SAY? DEAR OH DEAR. STILL, NEVER MIND, WORSE THINGS HAPPEN AT SEA

The king's corpse was loaded on to a cart by some peasants and it's said that blood dripped all the way to Winchester Cathedral where he was buried.

Little Hen

Name: Henry I 1068–1135
Claim to fame: William the Conqueror's youngest son. The first Norman king to be born in England.

Dreadful deeds: Henry was as ruthless as his dad. In 1090 he and his brother Robert went to war against their brother, William II. They captured one of William's knights called Conan and took him up the stairs of their castle tower. Conan begged them for mercy but the brothers just laughed. Henry had a nasty death planned for Conan. He threw him out of the window.

Henry later had trouble with Robert, and ended up locking him away for the rest of his life ... and Robert died in his Cardiff Castle prison at the age of 80.

Dire death: Henry's doctor warned him, 'Don't eat those eels, they're bad for you.' Henry ate the eels and had a nasty pain in the gut. The doctor advised, 'What you need is a laxative. It will give you diarrhoea for a day or so but it will clear out your bowels.' Sadly the doctor wasn't a very good doctor. He gave Henry a bit of an overdose. It gave him diarrhoea all right! And it killed him. What a way to go! Pooh!

Sad Steve

Name: Stephen 1097–1154

Claim to fame: Stephen battled for the throne of England with his cousin, Matilda, and brought misery to the whole country.

Dreadful deeds: Before Henry I was dead Stephen swore Henry's daughter (Matilda) could be the next queen of England. What did he do when Henry I died? Grabbed the throne for himself. (That's a bit of a surprise because

Stephen was a good fighter but a bit of a wimp. He was badly bossed about by his mum and his wife. They probably pushed his bum on to the throne of England. This must have been painful because Stephen had a nasty condition called 'piles' which gave him a sore bum.)

Anyway, Matilda was furious and invaded and so it went on. *Dire death:* Stephen, like William the Conqueror, fell ill with a pain in the guts. It was probably a burst appendix. Today that can still kill people but, if they can get to hospital in time, doctors can operate to cut it out. Stephen didn't have any slicing surgeons so he died in agony.

NORMAN NASTINESS

The Normans could be ruthless at times. (And if they set fire to the thatch on your cottage you'd be pretty roofless yourself!)

One of William the Conqueror's cruellest acts was known as 'The Harrying of the North' when he destroyed a whole region. Usually he was merciful to his defeated enemies. What drove him to this awful act?

Evil English in darkest Durham

It would be wrong to think the cruelty was all on the part of the Normans. The English could be pretty nasty when they wanted to be.

Just 60 years before the Battle of Hastings the northerners had beaten the Scots, cut off the best-looking heads and put them on show around the walls of Durham. The message was clear to anyone who wanted to take over – 'Nothing personal, Mr Conqueror. We don't like being ruled by *anybody*!'

In January 1069 the Normans took the city of Durham … for a while. If a monk had kept a personal diary of those dire days in Durham, it might have looked something like this.

> 30th day of January, the year of our Lord one thousand and sixty-nine.
>
> Today I went to the market-place and saw our conquerors. The man Robert of Comines marched into our city at dawn with his army of seven hundred men and put soldiers at every street corner. A few brave men tried to gather and

attack them but they were hacked down by the men in chain armour. The bodies are still in the narrow streets and their blood is trickling towards the River Wear but it is freezing in the gutters before it gets there.

Comines spoke to the crowd – he spoke french so only a few of us understood. 'I am here by the right of William of Normandy, King of England,' he told us. 'Anyone who refuses to obey an order from me or one of my men will be executed on the spot.' He turned to the Bishop of Durham, Aegelwine, and said, 'Make sure these ignorant English know what I said.'

Our Bishop clutched at his cross and said boldly, 'It will end in your defeat, my lord Comines. You will be thrown out of Durham.'

The Norman sneered and said, 'Talking of being thrown out, I am throwing you out of your palace. It will become my home while I am in Durham. You can sleep in the monastery.'

It is a sad day for Durham. But as we left the market-place we heard the people muttering. A rebel army is already gathering and will attack very soon. As a man of God I hate bloodshed – but the Normans need to be taught a lesson. Let us see what God brings us tomorrow.

———

31st day of January, the year of our Lord one thousand and sixty-nine

Oh the horror and the pity and the glory of it. Early this morning the rebel army arrived and before the Normans were awake they'd broken down our city gates. The people rose to join them armed with sickles and knives. The Normans tried to attack but they were trapped as soon as they entered the narrow city streets.

The Normans were hacked to the ground. The blood of yesterday's dead English was washed away by the blood of the Norman soldiers. When the Normans saw what was happening some fled to join Robert Comines in the Bishop's palace. But the mob set fire to the house.

'You'll set fire to our church!' I tried to tell them as the flames blew towards the Minster. Then God showed his glory as the wind changed and saved our lovely building. A miracle of God!

But nothing could save Comines and his cut-throat killers. They burned to death and I still hear their screams in my mind. But it is silent out there now. A light snow is falling to cover the Norman bodies.

Every last Norman is dead. Tonight we will pray that they never return.

In fact just two Norman soldiers managed to escape and take the shocking news back to William the Conqueror.

He was not pleased. Not one bit.

The magical mist

Of course the Normans *did* return, but again they failed to take Durham. This time the people of the city believed they were saved by a miracle…

15th day of September, the year of our Lord one thousand and sixty-nine

Since those blood-soaked days of January we have been steeling ourselves for the return of Duke William's armies. Messengers arrived three days ago to say they had set off from York and probably arrive today. All of yesterday we prayed in the Minster for God to spare us and today we heard our prayers have been answered.

A rider clattered into the market-place on his sweating horse, demanding to be taken to the bishop. I was sure that the news would be bad but I led him up the steep streets to the bishop's new house. I led the man in to Bishop Aegelwine and you cannot blame me if I stayed a little while to hear the news.

'Bishop,' the man cried. 'It's a miracle! The

Norman army reached Northallerton, barely a day's march from Durham, and they've turned back!'

The bishop nodded but argued, 'That is no miracle, my son.'

'But it is! As they set off a sudden fog descended on them from heaven. The Normans could not see the road ahead of them. They were terrified. They were sure that it was a sign.'

I hurried from the room with the news for my brothers who were in the Minster. I rested my hand on the coffin of our dear Saint Cuthbert and felt it chilly and damp as if it were covered in a mist. 'Saint Cuthbert has saved us!' I told them. 'Saint Cuthbert has sent a fog to confuse our enemies! We are saved!'

And today the word has spread through Durham. We have been saved by Cuthbert's miracle.

The truth is never that simple. A Danish army had landed on the coast just as the Normans set off from York to march on Durham. That was the *real* reason the Norman army turned back. The invasion had to be dealt with first.

The miraculous path

The people and the monks of Durham may have believed the miracle of Saint Cuthbert. But they were still sure the Normans would be back – and that their first victim would be the corpse of old Saint Cuthbert in Durham Minster.

So the monks decided to move the coffin further north to the safety of the island of Lindisfarne. The island is just off the Northumberland coast and when the monks arrived they could find no boat to take them across.

Then they looked in amazement as the waters fell away and a path appeared. It let them walk all the way to the island. The monks cried...

ANOTHER ONE OF SAINT CUTHBERT'S MIRACLES!

The truth is this path appears twice a day, every day, when the tide goes out!

The monks left the coffin in safety and returned to Durham and a nasty shock – their Bishop Aegelwine had run away and taken some of Durham's richest treasures with him!

CHEEKY MONKY

Wise man, Aegelwine. He knew that this time the Normans would return and take their revenge. He didn't want to be around when they did. They were about to begin...

The Harrying of the North

Some of the stories told about the Normans show that wherever they went the message was, 'You don't mess with a Norman'.

The Norman invasion of England in 1066 didn't put William's bum safely on the throne. The English weren't going to give up just because King Harold had been hacked at Hastings.

In 1069 the English revolted in the south while the warrior-leader Edric the Wild went wild in the west. In the north the Vikings crossed the North Sea to help Saxon Prince Edgar.

AND US NORTHERNERS WERE SO PLEASED TO SEE THEM WE JOINED OUR FRIENDS THE VIKINGS!

WE ARE A VERY FRIENDLY PEOPLE!

The Vikings marched on York. The Norman defenders set fire to the city and left the safety of York castle to fight the enemy in open battle. They were wiped out...

THE ONLY GOOD NORMAN IS A DEAD ONE, AS MY OLD DAD USED TO SAY

ACTUALLY HIS DAD USED TO SAY THAT ABOUT US VIKINGS!

The northern English towns and villages held fine fat feasts for the vicious Vikings. There were rumbles of rebellion in the rest of England.

William set off to sort out the nuisance in the north. He didn't just want to win. He wanted to destroy them so completely they would never rebel again. What he did became known as 'The Harrying of the North'.

The Vikings left York before William could catch them…

William set about destroying the northern region as he marched through it. Every English male was murdered.

The houses and the barns were burned. The farm animals were killed so there was nothing left for the people to eat.

Corpses were left to rot by the side of the roads and the desperate English survivors ate them to stay alive…

Horrible Histories Health Warning: Eating dead bodies you find in a ditch can damage your health. So don't do it.

Disease came along to add to the misery of the survivors. The northern towns and villages were still struggling to recover years later.

The North certainly didn't revolt again. The Conqueror's cruelty worked.

Twenty years after 'The Harrying of the North' William the Conqueror started to feel bad about his cruelty. It's said he was dead sorry … unlike the English who were simply dead dead.

The stuffed saint
When the Norman kingdom had settled, over 30 years later, they brought Cuthbert back to Durham to put him in the new cathedral the Normans were building there.

Before the body was moved to its new resting place the coffin was opened by ten monks. They reported that the body had not rotted and it smelled sweet!

It was 417 years old! Bet you don't look fresh and smell sweet when you're 417 years old!

A miracle? Or was the body mummified when it was first buried? Was the sweet smell the scent of the oils used?

The coffin can still be seen in Durham Cathedral today. But a) do not try to get into Cuth's coffin for a quick peek, and b) do not pour oil over your favourite granny in the hope she'll stay fresh for another 417 years!

Cuthbert appeared to have forgiven the Normans for disturbing his rest. There is a story that at the end of the 1100s the Norman Archbishop of York was seriously ill. The doctors said there was nothing they could do for him. Then he had a dream in which he was told to go to the tomb of Saint Cuthbert and sleep there. The Archbish did as he was told and ... Lo! He had a vision that old Cuth appeared and ran his hands over him. The Norman was cured immediately.

(Please note, that archbishop is now dead and has been for 800 years. Cuth's cure works once but you can't expect him to keep you going for ever.)

Whacking Walcher

The Normans gave all the top jobs in England to Norman lords. In the north the Bishop of Durham became a prince as well as a bishop. He ruled the church and the people.

The first Norman prince-bishop of Durham was William Walcher. It wasn't an easy job. English monks from a Tyneside monastery at Jarrow had to pick up the pieces of Walcher's last quarrel. If one of the young monks had written home, his letter may have described the event something like this…

16 May 1080

Dear Mum and Dad,

You never told me it was going to be so dangerous when you sent me to be a monk! Can't I come home now and work on the farm? I was in Gateshead this morning and you should see the mess! It was enough to make me sick. Far worse than slaughter-time on the farm each autumn. Let me tell you about it and then you can see why I want to come home.

You may remember Bishop Walcher was getting on quite well. He'd made a lot of friends with the great English families around here. And one of his best pals was Liulf of Lumley. Of course there were people jealous of Liulf weren't there? The ones who were most jealous were the bishop's own Norman friends. Especially that Gilbert!

That Gilbert was a monster! Worse

than William the Conqueror! You may have heard that Gilbert was so jealous of Liulf of Lumley he set off for the Lumley house and murdered him in his bed. Then he went off and tried to kill all of the rest of the Lumley family in their beds! He was wild as a fox in a chicken run.

Everybody blamed Bishop Walcher, didn't they? Gilbert was the bishop's man. There were riots up in Gateshead when the English heard about the Lumley murders. So the brave bishop said, 'Look, I'll come to a meeting with the Lumley family and make peace.'

'Yeah,' the Lumley family said. 'And make sure you bring your friend Gilbert with you!'

So off he went to Gateshead church. Naturally he had a hundred guards with him, but it didn't do him much good. You can imagine the mob that met them at the church! 'Kill the bishop! Kill the bishop!' they chanted.

Well, poor old Walcher fled into the church. But the mob forced him to send Gilbert outside to make peace. Make peace! They made pieces! Pieces of Gilbert! Bits of him in every corner of the churchyard.

And that's when they set fire to the church. The bishop staggered out, choking with the smoke. They say his eyes were so blinded by the smoke he couldn't see. Just as well, I suppose. Everybody in that English mob wanted to have a chop at him. He was a real mess.

I know this, Dad, because they sent us from Jarrow this morning to tidy up and give Walcher a Christian burial. We found his body, stripped of its prince-bishop robes, and we could hardly recognize it. Like I say, a real mess. We had to pick it up, put it on a cart and take it back with us.

A few of the mob came back to the ruined church and pelted us with mud. 'Let the crows have him!' they told us. I tell you, Dad and Mum, I've never been so scared in my life!

They say the murderers have fled to Scotland. But I can't do that, can I? Please can I come home?

Your loving son, Eadulf

Cropped coast

In 1085 William the Conqueror was back in Normandy when news arrived – England was about to be invaded. King Cnut of Denmark was teaming up with his son-in-law, Robert of Flanders. Together they'd fight for the English throne that Cnut believed should be his.

William gathered a huge army and shipped it across the English Channel. Reports at the time were sensational…

READ ALL ABAHT IT! CHANNEL FILLED WITH SHIPS THAT STRETCH FROM THE ENGLISH COAST TO THE NORMANDY COAST! READ ALL ABAHT IT!

NORMAN NEWS SHIPS SHORE TO SHORE

William wasn't sure where Cnut would land. He knew that an invading army could survive by looting the farms on the coast. So what did he do?

Answer:
William ordered that all the crops and stores of food along the English coast should be destroyed. The poor people who'd worked hard all year were moved inland for safety. The invasion never arrived so those farmers moved back to their homes by the coast … and hunger.

Caught red-handed

Bishop Odo of Bayeux was William the Conqueror's half-brother. In conquered England he acted as a judge and, with the help of a jury, decided arguments.

Being a member of a jury today means you have to be fair and honest. If you're not then you could go to prison. But prison isn't as bad as the punishment Odo saved for cheating jurymen in his day.

If there had been newspapers in Norman times then the case may have been reported like this …

English edition   Price: Half a dozen eggs

THE NORMAN NEWS

Jury Fury

Angry Odo

Bishop Odo gave the punishers some punishment today … and it didn't half hurt! Twelve members of the jury in the Islesham Manor Case have been found guilty of lying in court. Our readers will remember the case where the Bishop of Rochester and the Sheriff of Cambridge were arguing over who owned the stately home. The twelve good men and untrue of the jury decided to give it to the Sheriff.

That might have been an end to it but a Rochester monk made a sensational claim. The jury had not played fair, and, what's more, the mean monk could prove it!

Today Bishop Odo (The Basher Bishop, or Bish Bash as our readers know him) heard the evidence and decided the jury were indeed as bent as a nine-groat piece. First Bish Bash fined them till their purses were empty as Harold's eye-socket. Then he ordered that the guilty men should have their right hands plunged into boiling water.

Our ace reporter, Hugh Je Scoop, watched the sentence being carried out. 'I'd like to get my hand on the monk that fingered me,' muttered one victim (who wishes to remain nameless).

Juror in hot water

His wife Jeanne de Yorke (who also wishes to remain nameless) said, 'I told him that trying his hand at lying to Odo would get him in hot water. Once Odo takes matters in hand he always wins hands down. You have to hand it to him. Wasn't I right?'

NORMAN ITALY

The Norman control of Italy began almost by accident, probably around the year 999. Forty Norman pilgrims were returning from Jerusalem to Normandy and rested at Salerno in Southern Italy. While they were there the town was raided by Saracens. The Normans were shocked to see that the Salerno citizens did little to stop them.

The Normans went to Prince Gaimar of Salerno and said: 'Give us horses and weapons and we'll sort out these Saracens for you!'

The Normans drove the Saracens away and the prince was delighted. Prince Gaimar begged them to stay but they refused. The prince loaded them with gifts and sent more gifts back to Normandy to persuade other Normans to return. Prince Gaimar's message was:

> Come to this land that flows with milk and honey and so many beautiful things

Normans knights returned to Italy and set about the invaders from all sides. They drove Greek invaders from Apulia in the south-west of Italy. But which were worse for the Italians? Their Greek enemies or Norman 'friends'? As William of Apulia said at the time…

> *All the people of Apulia feared the Normans and many perished as the victims of their cruelty*

WHO ARE WE HARASSING TODAY?

DOES IT MATTER?

That's the Normans for you! Invite them in to help and they boss you about and beat you up. It's a bit like having burglars in your home and inviting bullies in to bash the burglars.

The Normans won five great victories in a row. But once the Greeks realized the power of the Normans they returned with a huge army to oppose them. The historian Amatus said…

October 1018
The Greeks swarmed over the battlefield of Ofanto like bees from an overflowing hive. Of 250 Normans only ten survived, the rest were cut to pieces.

The Normans didn't 'invade' Italy. They were just knights looking for a good fight. They'd fight for anybody who paid them. Some even joined the Greeks and fought against Normans who were on the side of Apulia. (At least they were kind to their Norman opponents when they defeated them!)

The heroic Hautevilles

And then along came the Hauteville brothers – all twelve of them. Once these battling boys arrived then the Normans started to take over southern Italy.

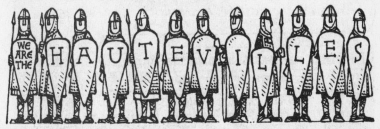

The Normans seemed to be outnumbered in every battle they fought, yet they always won. Sometimes they avoided fighting against huge numbers. Young William, for example, challenged the enemy leader to 'single combat' – one against one, a bit like a tennis match at Wimbledon only with a bit more blood.

WILLIAM KNOCKED ThE EMIR OFF HIS hORSE ThEN SLEW HIM. ....

A KNIGHT'S GOTTA DO WHAT A KNIGHT'S GOTTA DO!

FOR ThAT GREAT DEED ThE KNIGHT BECAME KNOWN AS WILLIAM IRON ARM.

AND MY HEAD IS PRETTY HARD TOO!

And remember when the Normans were massacred at Ofanto by the buzzing-bee Greeks? William Iron Arm went back to the same battlefield 23 years later (1041 if you're a dummy at summies). They say William Iron Arm had a terrible fever at the time but he won this return match.

CRAZY CRUSADERS

In 1096 the Pope asked Christians to go and capture the Holy Land from the Muslims. Of course the Normans were the first to join in. They'd had plenty of practice fighting Muslims in Italy. Now they had another excuse for a good fight.

Many knights fought in the Crusades because they were Christians or because they were serving their lord. But some knights were 'mercenary' and fought because they were paid to fight – 800 hyperperes for a knight and 400 for his squire. These mercenary knights had to work for their pay – or else. The punishment for a knight without fight could be to have his armour taken away. Still, that was better than being a cowardly ordinary soldier. He would have his hand pierced with a hot iron.

Did you know…?
Knightly Norman William de Perci had Whitby Abbey built. He then went off on Crusade, where he died. It is said his heart was brought back for burial at Whitby Abbey. Of course Whitby is where Count Dracula was later said to have arrived in England to go in search of fresh victims. Wonder if he had a munch on de Perci's blood pump?

Powerful Prester

In 1145 a bishop of Syria wrote a startling letter to the Pope…

Your Holiness,

I have wonderful news for your brave Crusaders. There are many Muslim states between you and the Holy Land. But there is one mighty Christian state beyond Persia which may well come to the aid of the Crusaders.

This state is ruled by a priest-king called Prester John. Prester John is a descendant of the three wise men who took gifts to the baby Jesus.

Prester John has already defeated the Muslims in Persia and his armies are heading towards us. Let us pray that he arrives in time to help our brave knights.

The Bishop of Syria

When the news reached the Pope, the Crusaders became excited by the idea of having such a powerful ally – even though no one had heard of him before 1145! The excitement grew when a letter arrived from Prester John himself.

The letter was a forgery – Prester John didn't exist!

Imagine you were the Pope and you received a letter which said…

Your Holiness

I am Prester John and I rule the lands beyond Persia. I try to rule as a good Christian even though I am the most powerful king on earth. I have seventy-two lesser kings who accept me as their leader.

My lands are so rich that there are no poor people in them. There is no lying, no stealing, no crime of any kind. Still, I do have a magical mirror in my palace and through it I can look into any part of my country. If there is any plotting going on then I know all about it.

I have magical jewels that can control how warm or cold the weather is and a church which can grow or shrink depending on how many people are in it.

I look foward to the day when you can visit my land and see these wonders and many more.

Your loyal Christian friend
Prester John.

Now, if you'd been the Pope you would take one look at the letter, say, 'Ho! Ho! Very funny!' and drop it into the nearest bin.

What did Pope Alexander III do? He wrote back to Prester John! This is a bit like writing to Father Christmas ... very nice for five-year-old children to believe. But the leader of the Western Christian Church? What a Popish plonker!

The seriously bad news was that an Eastern invader had indeed defeated the Muslims in Persia in the 1140s. But it wasn't a mighty Christian priest-king called Prester John. It was the ruthless Mongol warlord Kor-Khan and the coming of the Mongols was *not* good news for the Christians of Europe.

Gorgeous Saint George

Saint George was a hero to the Normans. Why? Because he was a great fighter, of course. The Normans loved fighters.

St George was also a Christian who died because of his faith. The Normans believed that anyone who died for being a Christian would go straight to heaven – that's why they were so eager to fight in the Crusades against the Muslims.

So, who was this St George and what happened to him? It's pretty gruesome, but it may be worth it to get that top spot up in heaven...

How to become a saint

In the AD 500s George had been a brilliant Roman soldier. He became a Christian and gave all his money away to the poor. When the Emperor Diocletian decided to exterminate the Christians, George was tortured.

Do you have a teacher for Religious Education? Do you

have a local vicar or priest? Do you even have someone in your class who is so good and holy they make you sick? Then this is your chance to do them a favour and make them a saint. All you have to do is copy what the Romans did to St George.

Make your own saint

For this you need a really holy person and a lot of patience.

1. First lay your saint on the ground. Cover her/him with stones then larger rocks and finally get a few little boulders and pile them on until s/he is crushed. If your saint is truly a saint then s/he will survive. So...

 2. Take a wheel covered in spikes and roll it to the top of a steep hill. Tie your saint to the wheel and roll it down the hill. Just like Jack and Jill but a bit bloodier. If your saint is truly a saint then s/he will survive. So...

3. Take a pair of iron shoes and heat them till they are red hot. Put them on the feet of your saint and set her/him off to run in them. They'll set off hot foot, you can be sure. If your saint is truly a saint then s/he will survive. So...

4. Tie your saint to a cross, facing the cross. Take leather whips with knots in the end and a team of whippers. Whip the saint till their skin is hanging off their body. If your saint is truly a saint then s/he will survive. So...

5. Dig a deep pit in the ground. Throw your saint into the pit and cover her/him with quicklime (calcium oxide if you want the posh word). This will burn off their flesh till they're skinny as a skeleton key. If your saint is truly a saint then s/he will survive. So...

6. Get a bottle of poison at your local chemist shop. Slip the poison into your saint's tea and watch them drink the poison. If your saint is truly a saint then s/he will survive. So...

7. Behead your saint. That's what Diocletian did and it finally killed off Georgie.

But before he died – and in between the tortures – George...
- chatted to an angel
- raised dozens of people from the dead
- raised an ox from the dead
- converted the Emperor's wife to Christianity (she got the chop too, by the way!)
- converted 40,900 other people
- had the Emperor carried away by a whirlwind of fire

Whatever happened to the dragon?
Bet you thought Saint George was a saint because he slew a dragon? The Saint George that the Normans loved never did that. The dragon only appears in the book *Golden Legend*, written in the late 1200s. So now you know.

Horrible for horses
Life in the Norman world could be awful for horses. Especially when they went into battle...
- The charge of Norman knights was a fearsome thing, but the Muslim warriors found a way to stop it. They used their arrows and javelins to bring down the horses. Once the horse fell then the knight could be battered senseless.

One knight, de Joinville, was hit by five arrows – but his poor horse was hit by 15 and fell. Later that year de Joinville had a spear thrust through his leg. It also stuck firmly in the neck of his horse and pinned him there. This was a bit of a pain in the neck for both of them!

- An Italian historian, Amatus, described a Norman duke as follows...

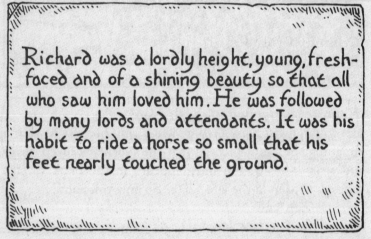

'All who saw him loved him'? I'll bet the little horses in Italy didn't love him! 'Oh, no!' they must have whinnied when they saw him coming. 'Why can't he pick on some horse his own size?'

- Horses are reasonable swimmers. They can even swim with a rider on their back. But it's a bit much to ask a horse to swim with a heavy war saddle and a rider with chain-mail armour, iron helmet and battle sword. That's what the knights expected from their horses after the battle of Val-es-Dunes in 1047. Not only did the riders drown (which served them right) but they took the poor horses down with them. A writer who visited the battlefield said…

The water-mills of Borbillon had their wheels clogged with the bodies.

Crummy Crusades

By the middle of the 1200s the Crusades were not so popular. The religious writer, Humbert of Romans, said…

Priests who call for a Crusade are mocked these days. And the knights who sign up to go are usually drunk at the time!

There were eight Crusades lasting almost 200 years. The Christians won a few battles and captured a few towns but, in the end, they left the Holy Land in defeat.

Still, the Normans got most of what they wanted from the Crusades – an exciting punch-up, a bit of glory … and a ticket to their Christian heaven. What more would a Norman knight need?

MISCHIEVOUS MONKS

The Normans set up hundreds of monasteries wherever they went in Normandy, Italy, the Holy Land and England. Men and women flocked to become monks and nuns, but not every one was a saint – not every religious place was holy.

Wholly holy

Abbot Ailred was in charge of Rievaulx Abbey in Yorkshire (founded in 1131). When he died monks wrote his story and didn't forget to praise themselves!

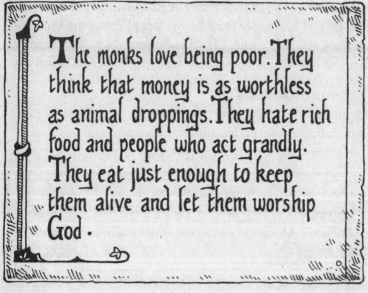

The monks love being poor. They think that money is as worthless as animal droppings. They hate rich food and people who act grandly. They eat just enough to keep them alive and let them worship God.

Sounds a pretty boring sort of life really. But of course not all monks were as goody-goody as that …

Not wholly holy

Gerald of Wales (1146–1223) said that the monasteries could be very ungodly places.

1 Wealth

> *They got lands by acting like saints and using 'God' as every other word.*

So, the monks just *appeared* to be holy so they could get their hands on lands.

Interesting thought, using 'God' as every other word! That would mean if they read the Ruth chapter of the Bible that says 'Thy people shall be my people, and thy God my God', it would become: 'Thy God people God shall God be God my God people God and God thy God God God my God God God.'

2 Land

> *Once they get land they waste no time in putting it to use. The woods are cut down and levelled into a plain, bushes give way to barley and willows to wheat. They flatten villages, overthrow churches, turn villagers on to the roads and don't hesitate to cast down altars and level all under the plough.*

I CAN FLATTEN ANYTHING. I'VE GOT A BULLDOZER

THAT'S NOTHING, I'VE GOT A MONASTERY

Gerald went on to say that if a man invited the monks on to part of his land, they ended up throwing him out of the rest. 'The coming of Cistercian monks is worse than the coming of a war.' Today he might have said a bit like motorway builders – except he isn't alive today and the Normans didn't have motorways.

3 Ruthlessness

The most amazing story was of a knight who refused to give up his land to the monks of Byland Abbey. Walter Map, a Welsh writer of the time, described what happened next...

One night they entered his house with masks over their faces, armed with swords and spears, and they murdered him and his family. When his relations arrived three days later they found the houses and barns had all disappeared and in their place was a well-ploughed field.

BYLAND ABBEY?

THIEVELAND ABBEY. MORE LIKE!

Sort of, 'Night-night, knight!'

4 Simple food

Then there was the rule that the monks should eat simple food and be silent during meals. If they wanted to ask for salt or water then they used one of the hundred signs they had.

St Bernard of Clairvaux was horrified by what he saw at Canterbury…

> *As to the dishes and the number of them – what shall I say? I have often heard sixteen or more costly dishes were placed on the table. Many kinds of fish (roast and boiled, stuffed and fried) many dishes created with eggs and pepper by skilful cooks and so on! The meal was washed down with wine, claret, mead and all drinks that can make a man drunk. The rule of silence did not prevent monks from showing their pleasure with signs that made them look more like jesters or clowns than monks. They were all waving with fingers, hands and arms and whistling to one another instead of speaking.*

And you thought your school dining-hall was bad with mashed potato and school bags flying around? Canterbury must have looked and sounded like a meeting of football referees! If St Bernard had his way they'd all have been shown a red card. (St Bernard was a true monk and gave away everything he possessed. He even gave his name to a dog!)

5 Little food
Not all monks got away with this good living. Gerald of Wales tells of the monks of St Swithuns, Winchester…

The monks had a good excuse for having so much food. They said they gave away their left-over food to the poor. The more dishes the monks were given the more scraps there were for the poor!

Nice try, boys.

Horrible Histories Health Warning: Do not believe everything you read in history books. Gerald of Wales twice applied to become Bishop of St David's in Wales. In both cases the monks persuaded the king not to give Gerald the job. In both cases the job went to a monk. Gerald had good reason to hate monks. His stories must have been written with a bit of spite.

6 Women

The Bible says, 'All wickedness is little compared to the wickedness of a woman.' (Female readers, don't write and complain to me. I didn't say it. Write to God.) Monks were expected to keep away from them.

Now if you are a monk then there is one sure way to lose interest in women. Don't let your naughty bits get over-heated. How do you keep them cool? Do not wear any underpants. And good Cistercian monks wore no underpants.

But this created other problems. One day King Henry II was riding through a town when a Cistercian monk stumbled, trying to get out of his way. The monk fell flat on his face and his robe blew over his head. The king said nothing but a priest who was riding with the king said…

Cursed be the Cistercians who show their backsides.

No doubt the monk's cheeks turned red with embarrassment … the cheeks of his face, of course. What did you think I meant?

Did you know… ?
When a boy joined a monastery at the age of seven he was given a monk's robes and a monk's hair cut. But there was

117

one thing he didn't get until he became an adult monk at the age of 16. What was it?

Gerry's Welsh wonder

Gerald of Wales wrote a book about his travels through Wales in 1188. He tells a story that probably doesn't belong in a travel book...

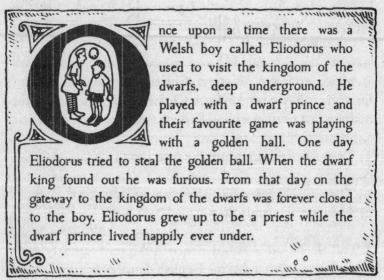

nce upon a time there was a Welsh boy called Eliodorus who used to visit the kingdom of the dwarfs, deep underground. He played with a dwarf prince and their favourite game was playing with a golden ball. One day Eliodorus tried to steal the golden ball. When the dwarf king found out he was furious. From that day on the gateway to the kingdom of the dwarfs was forever closed to the boy. Eliodorus grew up to be a priest while the dwarf prince lived happily ever under.

Yes, Gerald, and there are fairies at the bottom of our garden.

NORMAN QUIZ

1 A knight who upset his leader could be punished with his own horse. How?

a) He was forced to trot along a road in full armour on his horse.

b) He was tied to the tail of the horse and had to run behind it or be dragged.

c) He was forced to eat it … raw … without salt, pepper or mustard. Not even a cup of tea to wash it down with.

I THINK THAT ONE'S A BIT TOO RAW

BAP!

CRASH!

2 Normans were Western Christians and during the Crusades they met Eastern Christians. Crusaders were discouraged from marrying Eastern Christian women. What happened to them if they did?

a) They were banished to the desert with just a camel for company.

b) They lost their armour which was melted down.

c) They lost the lands they owned back home.

3 The Scots did a sword dance – skipping quickly over sharp swords. What did the English dance over?

a) Smouldering coals.

b) Eggs.

c) Slithering snakes.

OI! WATCH IT, TWINKLE TOES!

4 Crusaders faced a dreadful weapon in the Middle East: 'Greek Fire'. It caught alight as soon as it touched sea water and threatened their ships. How did Norman crusaders fight Greek Fire?

a) With pee.

b) With spit.

c) They dialled 999 and let the Phrygian Fire-fighters fight it.

5 What was the Norman punishment for murder?

a) Hanging by the neck till dead.

b) Having your eyes put out.

c) Beheading (with a blunt axe).

6 Saint Godric died in 1170 at the age of 105. What did he do before he became a hermit monk and a saintly man?

a) He was a pie seller.

b) He was a pirate.

c) He was a pilot.

7 William the Conqueror knew he was dying in 1087, so he left his kingdom to…

a) His wife – but he was so ill he'd forgotten she was dead.

b) His son William Rufus (who became William II).

c) God.

8 What was the first thing William did when he jumped ashore at Hastings?

a) Fell flat on his face.

b) Fell down on his knees to pray.

c) Fell about laughing when he heard King Harold was 300 miles away.

9 Abbot Thurstan became the new Norman boss at Glastonbury but upset the monks there. The monks argued with Thurstan. What did he do?

a) He was so upset he jumped off the bell tower to his death.

b) He sent in Norman soldiers to slit a few monks' throats.

c) He prayed for a miracle and God sent angels to talk to the monks.

10 A Norman knight swore to prove his love for a lady. She told him to go off and pick up all the stones on the beaches of Brittany. What did he do?

a) Collected an army to do the job and won the heart of the lady.

b) Tried to do it himself but hurt his back and never fought again.

c) Sulked and went to bed for two years.

fig 1. a dark knight

Answers:

1 a) Trotting on a war-horse in full armour was painful. Knights walked to the battlefield and then set off at a canter into the charge. And they didn't gallop into the charge (the way you see in films). Some horses would go faster than others and the line would not be straight. The idea was to hit the enemy as a single block – a bit like the charge of pupils from the school gates at holiday time!

2 c) This didn't happen to all Norman knights but generally it was a bad idea to fall for an Eastern Christian woman, even if she was as pretty as a pot-bellied pig. Still, it could have been worse. A Greek knight who married an Eastern Christian woman could lose a hand or a foot.

3 b) The English danced over eggs. Not so brave as the Scots – unless there's a very angry hen in the room. You may like to try this in the kitchen. Place half a dozen eggs on the floor, turn on the radio and dance around. Too easy, you say? Fine! Try it blindfolded.

4 a) The recipe for Greek Fire has been lost since it was used in the Middle Ages. We can't test the fire-fighting methods to see if they'd work. But the Normans *believed* that throwing sand over the Greek Fire or pouring pee on it was the best way to kill the flames. That is not to say they stood there and risked singeing their piddling bits. If they expected an attack of Greek Fire they'd collect barrels of the stuff. Let's hope they didn't mix them up with the wine barrels.

5 b) The Normans were cruel but they rarely gave the death sentence to criminals. Prison was only used to hold criminals until their trial. A murderer might lose his hands or his eyes. Having your eyes put out was also the punishment for killing one of William the Conqueror's deer. Does that mean a human life was worth no more than the life of a deer?

6 b) Godric was born in Norfolk the year before William the Conqueror invaded. He grew up to be a pedlar – a sort of travelling salesman. Then he became a sea pirate. When his voyages took him as a pilgrim to Compostella in Spain he saw how wicked he'd been. 'I don't want to join a monastery,' he decided. 'I want to live a holy life alone ... as a hermit.' He had a fun life in a cave but was driven out by wolves. He finally settled into a specially built hermitage that the Normans built for him. See? You too can have a specially built council house if you're a good boy.

7 c) William hadn't inherited the crown of England from a father who had been king before him, so people could argue that there was no reason why his son should become the new king. Also he'd taken it in battle with a lot of blood spilt. That wouldn't look too good when he arrived at the gates of Heaven, would it?

'What have you done on earth, William?'

'Caused a few thousand bloody deaths!'

'Then go to hell!'

So William said, 'I leave my kingdom to God … and I hope God will give it to my second son, William.'

God didn't appear to argue.

8 a) William landed and stumbled. 'Ooooh!' his followers gasped. 'That's a bad sign!' But clever Will grabbed a handful of sand and said, 'See! I've already seized Harold's land!'

9 b) Thurstan sent for soldiers so the monks locked themselves in the monastery church. The soldiers easily broke down the door. Three of the monks rushed to the altar to pray – that didn't alter their fate. They were hacked to death. Many of the other monks were wounded as the soldiers lashed out.

10 c) The knight had asked for it really. Never ask a lady, 'What can I do to win your love?' She may not want her love to be won and might set an impossible task! It's much more simple to say, 'Do you fancy going to the pictures with me?'

EPILOGUE

The fashion at the first millennium was for men to have hair to their shoulders and long moustaches. The Normans cut their hair short and shaved their faces (except the women who didn't cut their hair short or shave their faces). To their enemies the Normans must have looked like skinheads!

And they behaved like skinheads too. They got what they wanted by being violent and they grew to enjoy fighting. (This was before television was invented, so they had to do something to pass the time.)

Of course the Normans had the perfect excuse ...

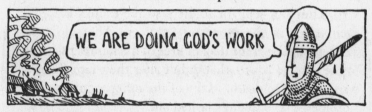

You may like to try this excuse some time ...

Of course you might be punished! Most people believe we should stand up to bullies like the Normans. (So, in 1999, when Serb bullies barged into Kosovo other countries joined forces to stop them.)

The Normans, like their Viking ancestors, were fearless fighters. They charged around Europe and changed it for ever. Why did they do it?

Italian historian Geoffrey Malaterra said…

They are passionate about wealth and power, yet they despise it when they have it. They are always looking for more.

Greedy, nasty Normans.

English Historian William of Malmesbury summed them up like this…

They are proudly dressed and delicate about their food — but not too much. They are jealous of their equals — and always want to do better than their superiors. They rob their subjects — yet they defend them against others. They are faithful to their lords — yet the slightest insult makes them wicked. They are only treacherous when they think they can get away with it.

They probably weren't nice to know, but they were the sort of people who would survive in today's world.

But did the Normans really win?

When French King Philip II took Normandy in 1204, the Normans in England had to choose – should they stay and become English? Or join the French to keep their Norman lands but lose their English ones? They stayed in England.

Some historians say this means the English won – the English didn't become Normans – the Normans became English!

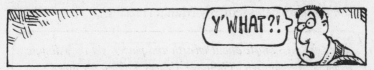

It's a horrible historical world where winners are losers and losers end up winners.

Now why not visit
www.terry-deary.com